# THE CREATION OF THE SELF AND LANGUAGE

# THE CREATION OF THE SELF AND LANGUAGE

## Primitive Sensory Relations of the Child with the Outside World

*David Rosenfeld*

Foreword by
*Maria Rhode*

KARNAC

First published in 2012 by
Karnac Books
118 Finchley Road
London NW3 5HT



**British Library Cataloguing in Publication Data**

A C.I.P. for this book is available from the British Library

ISBN: 978–1–78049–135–6

Edited, designed, and produced by Communication Crafts

Printed in Great Britain

www.karnacbooks.com

*This book is dedicated to the people*
*who encouraged me to write it:*
*my friends Carlos and Popi Abolsky*
*and my colleague Maria Rhode*

# Contents

## II
## Benjamin

# About the Author

**David Rosenfeld** was trained in Buenos Aires. He lived and studied in Paris and London and also in the United States. He is a Consultant Professor at Buenos Aires University, Faculty of Medicine, in the Department of Mental Health and Psychiatry; a Training Analyst of the Buenos Aires Psychoanalytic Society; and an Ex-Vice President of the International Psychoanalytical Association (IPA).

# Foreword

*Maria Rhode*

The publication of this book with its accompanying DVD is an important event. Karnac Books have made it possible for us to witness what David Rosenfeld's treatment of Benjamin, a young boy with a diagnosis of autism, was actually like. We can see for ourselves what was done, what was said; we can follow the steps by which Benjamin moved from being a child without language, in a state of perpetual panic-stricken screaming and flailing about, to being a "real kid" with friendships, doing well at an ordinary school. Witnessing this transformation is a profoundly moving experience. So is hearing

---

Maria Rhode is Emeritus Professor of Child Psychotherapy at the Tavistock and Portman NHS Foundation Trust.

the testimony of Benjamin's parents, who had been told repeatedly that there was no future for their son. It was their wish that his therapy should be more widely known about, in the hope that professionals could learn from it so that other families' lives might be transformed as theirs had been through "Dr David's" intervention. Everyone concerned with children with autism is in their debt.

Benjamin was given a diagnosis of autism by a university department of paediatric neurology. His problems had become evident when he was about 2½ years old, after his parents had become distraught with grief and anxiety upon discovering that their daughter, who was 6 years old, had been abused.

The whole family was involved in the subsequent treatment, with Benjamin's sister often serving as his interpreter before he could communicate more clearly himself. The treatment was highly emotionally charged: particularly in the beginning, it proved impossible to film some of the sessions because the impact on those involved was so great.

David Rosenfeld has long been renowned for his psychoanalytic work with psychotic adults, especially for his elucidation of aspects of their body image. Other contributions include a description of how precious experiences from the past can be "encapsulated" in the minds of Holocaust survivors and, in this way, be preserved until such time as circumstances make it possible to retrieve and re-integrate them. In 1996, he received the Mary S. Sigourney award for outstanding contributions to psychoanalysis. Readers of his papers, and of the two books in which some of the papers have been collected, will remember the delicacy of his approach to highly distressed patients, his ability to apprehend the nuances of their experience, and his capacity to talk with them in ways that make them realize they are no longer alone. When a psychotic young man whose family had been brutally traumatized during the Argentinian military dictatorship throws furniture and other objects around the consulting room, Rosenfeld speaks to him about how, as a toddler, he had felt that his mind was fragmented and reduced to chaos by the terrible things that had happened. All these qualities are brought to bear in his treatment of Benjamin.

The work shown on this DVD has many implications. First among these is the fact that a boy diagnosed with autism by a university department of paediatric neurology became capable of "normal" functioning. When psychoanalytic workers such as Frances Tustin have documented important improvements in children with autism, the objection has always been raised that they must have been misdiagnosed. In the absence of randomized controlled outcome studies, filmed documentation of the therapy process is of paramount importance. David Rosenfeld's films stand with Anni Bergman's as evidence of what a psychoanalytic approach to autism can achieve.

Professionals of all orientations increasingly agree that the behaviours on which a diagnosis of autism rests can come about through many different pathways. Workers interested in variations in these behaviours will find much to study in the DVD. So too will those concerned with the theory of technique in view of Rosenfeld's involvement of the whole family, the nature of his interventions, and his use of play materials. But perhaps what comes across most vividly is the quality of the therapeutic atmosphere. The moment when Benjamin, playing with water, first uses a word, "water", which he repeats after Rosenfeld, brings to mind Helen Keller's recognition of the link between the word for water and the feel of water on her hand, which opened up for her the whole symbolic realm. The viewer of the DVD is in no doubt that it is the quality of the emotional link with his analyst that allowed Benjamin to take this step.

In addition, this book contains Rosenfeld's conceptualization of Benjamin's developing sense of self and his acquisition of language. In these chapters, Rosenfeld makes links between his psychoanalytic work with Benjamin and seminal ideas from other disciplines, such as those of the philosopher Maurice Merleau-Ponty and the psychologist Henri Wallon. More particularly, he offers a highly original discussion of language acquisition in relation to Freud's paper on aphasia. These theoretical sections will be of special interest to psychoanalysts and child psychotherapists, who will also find much to study in the DVD that can help to answer the vital question of which children with autism can benefit from a psychoanalytic approach. Psychiatrists, teachers, social workers, and parents—indeed, anyone involved with children like Benjamin—will also find much to interest them in this book, which, I have no doubt, will have an important influence on the future direction of work with children on the autistic spectrum.

PART I

# THE AUTISTIC CHILD

*The treatment of an autistic child is an opportunity to observe and to investigate the origins of verbal symbols and language creation, as well as how the logic of thought is constructed.*

# 1

# Introduction

In this book, I develop models and hypotheses about the mechanisms of the origin of language and the self, along the following lines:

1. A return to Freud for a theoretical review of autistic mechanisms
2. The concept of self
3. The possible disappearance of introjections
4. The concept of body image
5. Autistic encapsulation to achieve preservation
6. Treatment technique
7. Four years of filming

## A return to Freud for a theoretical review of autistic mechanisms

In his "Project for a Scientific Psychology", Freud (1950 [1895]) describes how the first contact of the child with the outside world—as in the case of a baby at his mother's breast—is of a sensory nature. As I show below, the first hallucination is a repetition of this early sensory feeling: the mouth on the breast.

When we watch a baby moving his mouth, imagining he is suckling at the breast, this hallucination—"the first psychological mechanism"—is also a "communication". The communication will only be useful if it is interpreted—in other words, if the message is received and understood by the mother.

Here I emphasize (and I deliberately underscore) that, without sensory contact with an object, the child cannot link the sensory contact to the verbal symbol, as was the case with Benjamin, the child in my office: each time he touched water, I named it for him, and I said the word "water". And that was the first word Benjamin uttered, but it only happened after he actually *felt* the water, with his sense of touch, and played with it together with the therapist.

We therefore come back to Freud's first postulates on relationships with the outside world through sensory contact. I also address the same issue in chapter 4, which is devoted to Merleau-Ponty and Henri Wallon.

The first sensory contacts can sometimes be

hallucinated, and it is important to highlight once again that these bodily sensory impressions are key, since, for Freud, the body is also the I, the Ego, the Me. Also importantly, Frances Tustin (1986, 1990) writes that when the autistic child is trapped in his own sensory feelings, his relationship to the real outside world is blocked, both preventing him from communicating and blocking the introjection and projective identification that are needed to communicate.

The first hallucination is mentioned in Volume 5 of *The Interpretation of Dreams* (1900), and I emphasize that, for Freud, hallucination is not visual or auditory, but sensory, tactile: the baby's suckling, imagining his mother's breast, is a tactile hallucination, considered as the first psychic mechanism. The following quote is from Freud's "Project for a Scientific Psychology" (1950 [1895], p. 318):

> It takes place by *extraneous help*, when *the attention of an experienced person is drawn to the child's state by discharge along the path of internal change* [emphasis added]. In this way this path of discharge acquires a secondary function of the highest importance, that of *communication*, and the initial helplessness of human beings is the *primal source* of all *moral motives*.
>
> When the helpful person has performed the work of the specific action in the external world for the helpless one, the latter is in a position, by means of reflex contrivances, immediately to carry out in the interior of his body the activity necessary for removing the endogenous stimulus. The

> total event then constitutes an *experience of satisfaction*, which has the most radical results on the development of the individual's functions.[1]

Freud (1900, p. 566) writes that the first properly psychic activity is likely to have been hallucination. Primitive hallucination—which Freud considers the first mental mechanism—is, I believe, related to autistic mechanisms.

Freud describes a hallucination that is tactile and sensory (he does not say visual or auditory). Based on this model, I think that the autistic child returns to the first impression of his psychic mechanism: primitive hallucination.

The autistic child envelops and surrounds himself with this sensory impression.

For the treatment of these children, we must make a journey that is the opposite of regression and go through the normal developmental mechanisms described by Freud.

---

[1]The quotation continues as follows:

> For three things occur in the ψ system: (1) a lasting discharge is effected and so the urgency which had produced unpleasure in ϖ is brought to an end; (2) a cathexis of one (or several) of the neurones which correspond to the perception of an object occurs in the pallium; and (3) at other points of the pallium information arrives of the discharge of the released reflex movement which follows upon the specific action. A facilitation is then formed between these cathexes and the nuclear neurones.
>
> The information of the reflex discharge comes about because every movement, through its subsidiary results, becomes the occasion for fresh sensory excitations (*from the skin and muscles*) [emphasis added], which give rise to a motor (kinesthetic) image in ψ.

## The concept of self

The concept of self is a creation in ongoing development. It is a dialectic process.

In a letter sent by Winnicott to his French translator, Jeannine Kalmanovitch, he wrote:

> For me the self, which is not the ego, is the person who is me, who is only me, who has a totality based on the operation of the maturational process. At the same time the self has parts, and in fact is constituted of these parts. These parts agglutinate from a direction interior–exterior in the course of the operation of the maturational process, aided as it must be (maximally at the beginning) by the human environment which holds and handles and in a live way facilitates. The self finds itself naturally placed in the body, but may in certain circumstances become dissociated from the body or the body from it. The self essentially recognises itself in the eyes and facial expression of the mother and in the mirror which can come to represent the mother's face. Eventually the self arrives at a significant relationship between the child and the sum of the identifications which (after enough of incorporation and introjection of mental representations) become organised in the shape of an internal psychic living reality. The relationship between the boy or girl and his or her own internal psychic organisation becomes modified according to the expectations that are displayed by the father and mother and those who have become significant in the external life of the individual. It is the self and the life of the self that alone makes sense of action or of living from the point of view of the

> individual who has grown so far and who is continuing to grow from dependence and immaturity towards independence, and the capacity to identify with mature love objects without loss of individual identity. [1970, p. 271]

Ludwig Haesler (2010), in a paper presented at the 5th Frances Tustin Memorial Conference in Berlin, describes the difficulty of the never-ending creation of the self.

## The possible disappearance of introjections

Introjections, or introjective identifications, are not fixed or stable. In cases of severe trauma, they may disappear. This is a "strong theory". Having had the opportunity to treat patients who were survivors of Nazi persecution, I postulate that introjections—the bonds and the language of childhood—may disappear (Rosenfeld, 1986).

I must emphasize strongly: nothing is totally stable, everything is mobile and changes, and this can be seen either after very severe trauma or in extremely sensitive children, such as autistic children.

## The concept of body image

This model develops in parallel with the concept of self. Body image is gradually created according to (1) cultural codes, (2) family influences, and (3) the unconscious phantasies of the subject him/herself.

## Autistic encapsulation to achieve preservation

The fundamental theory on which I base the treatment of autistic children is that of autistic encapsulation to achieve the preservation of healthy bonds from early childhood (see chapter 2).

## Treatment technique

The treatment is based, as postulated by Freud, on evolving from perception (sensory functions) and later reaching the motor pole (Freud, 1900, p. 537).

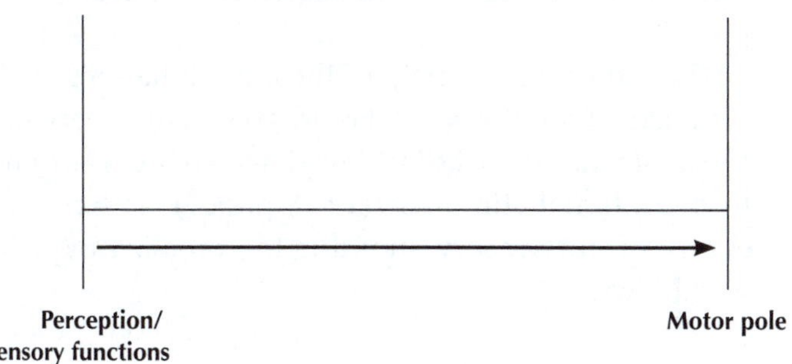


## Four years of filming

In part II, I present excerpts from four years of filmed sessions with an autistic boy, Benjamin, along with descriptions of them based on transcripts of the sessions.

During Benjamin's four years of treatment—summarized on the DVD in the 45-minute video entitled *"Now I Am a Real Kid"*—I tried to recuperate language following the developmental path described by Freud. To quote: "Impulse will at once emerge, seeking to *re-cathect* the mnemic image and re-evoke the perception itself" (Freud, 1926 [1925], p. 75).

In other words, words are recathected and recovered, as illustrated in the video, where, with the therapist's help, the patient can connect the sensory function (touching the water with his hand) with vocalization of the word "water"—the first word the patient recovers. And I again quote Freud: "A change can only come about . . . through outside help" (1900, p. 565).

Thus, through the help of the Other, the sensory is connected with the word. Freud says: "An experience of satisfaction can be achieved which puts an end to the internal stimulus" (1900, p. 565). The patient evolves from sensory stimulus to verbalization (the word "water").

# 2

## Revisiting Freud from the standpoint of his writings on aphasia

In his work on aphasia, Freud interprets mental space through language and representation levels (Freud, 1891, 1911; Grubrich-Simitis, 2003).

Although the loss of language in the autistic child is not exactly a neurological aphasia, it is possible to formulate a hypothesis according to which the therapist achieves the recuperation of words via sensory stimulus by naming each object as the subject touches it with his or her hand or tongue.

Ricardo Avenburg (1974, 1995) considers that aphasias reproduce a state that existed in the normal course of learning to speak: when the child learns to read and to write, he tries to appropriate for himself the visual image of the word, evoking all the other acoustic and kinaesthetic images associated to that image (Avenburg, personal communication, 2010).

I personally emphasize, with Tustin (1986, 1990), the sensory contact with the lips and the mouth's mucosa, as can be seen in the video, *Now I Am a Real Kid*.

Our task as psychoanalysts is to recreate the mental apparatus and language. We know today that brain functions and the connections of neural dendrites can be amplified and recreated, as is shown in the research of Dr Levy Montalcini (2009), winner of the 1986 Nobel Prize for Medicine. It is interesting to rethink aphasias as an interruption of associations; in the autistic child, there is also an interruption of language.

In the video, the representation of the self is especially associated with language. Once the boy can look and uses his vision, distal perception provides him with 3D vision outside and inside himself.

Avenburg (1995) states that "In the childhood phase of language development we use a language built by ourselves, by associating other different sounds of words to the one we produce: we behave like motor aphasics" (p. 75).

Note in the video how, when the autistic encapsulation that preserves and maintains the healthiest aspects of childhood begins to open, we can see that it has also preserved the language learned before the age of 3½ years, and all the prior aspects then emerge, perfectly preserved.

This is what I could observe with survivors of Nazi persecution,[1] who kept the language of their childhood, which they had thought was lost for ever, preserved by the mechanism of autistic encapsulation. Thus, forty years later, during a therapy session, a patient starts singing in German, and another patient suddenly remembers his childhood name in Italian (Rosenfeld, 1986; see also Ferrari, 1987; Grotstein, 1978; Haesler, 1992; Houzel, 2000; Houzel & Bursztejn, 2000; Nissen, 2006; Rosenfeld, 1992, 2006).

It was these patients who led me to discover how autistic encapsulation could be used to "preserve" infantile and healthy bonds from infancy and childhood, as well as language. Some of these patients have been able to use the powerful mechanism of autistic encapsulation inside the mind to preserve those bonds and that language.

I present below two dialectic poles: (1) the mechanism of autistic encapsulation; and (2) the disappearance of all introjections after a severe trauma.

This model of autistic encapsulation, used to preserve an aspect of the infantile self possessing good childhood bonds, is the key theory I used in the work with my patient, Benjamin.

---

[1]This should on no account be misunderstood as meaning that children develop autism because of being exposed to situations similar to those in the concentration camps. My point is purely that the mechanism of encapsulation can be used to preserve precious aspects of experience.

We began filming based on a firm theoretical idea (and I do mean firm, not rigid): to film for several years to see if I could find in the boy some healthy aspects from his first three years of life. This patient's condition had been triggered when he was 3 years old and had then become more severe, and it was therefore possible that autistic mechanisms had preserved his earlier, healthier infantile bonds.

The theory informing my investigation was therefore that of autistic encapsulation (Rosenfeld, 2006). It was possible that we might find what had been kept inside the mind, protected and preserved by his autistic mechanism.

Based on this hypothesis and this theoretical model, I began filming and working, trying to reconstruct the patient's symbolic system, his language and his mind.

I filmed, waiting to see what we would find, knowing basically nothing, with the objective of investigating and learning.

And here I address you—psychoanalysts, psychotherapists, and future psychoanalysts. Remember that the world of autism is an unknown world, a world full of anguish, a fantastic and dangerous world. To enter it, the first thing that you need to have is curiosity. You must not be frightened at the journey to the galaxies and into the unknown. You need curiosity, good teachers, and good company.

Every time Benjamin touched an object, a word was mentioned: it was named by the psychoanalyst.

And so was born the beginning of symbolization through the word. Being able to create a word means creating the symbolic device, creating the mind.

There is a beautiful scene with the patient, who doesn't speak yet, where he takes his sister's hand to show her a cartoon, and the sister says: "Camel". This is an example of a symbiosis that is useful for development. This anecdotal scene of the patient with his sister is extremely important, because he asks for her help to begin the symbolization process through the word.

# 3

# Some modern psychoanalytic theories on autism

I develop here the theories of Frances Tustin (1986, 1990), as discussed by Sheila Spensley (1995).

Like Margaret Mahler, Tustin views autism as a sensation-dominated state of being, with an accompanying impoverishment of emotional contact. Mahler stressed the importance of bodily sensations as the "crystallization point of the 'feeling of self', around which a 'sense of identity' will become established" (Mahler, Pine, & Bergman, 1975, p. 47). A sensory–emotional conjunction is required for sensation states to make way for feeling states. Normally, this takes place within the context of the earliest relationship with the child's caregiver. However, many children who later develop autism may avoid contact from the beginning, or their signals may be difficult to read, so that devoted parents find themselves unable to get through to them.

Mahler saw the necessity of a symbiotic experience from which the psychological birth takes place, enabling the infant to enter into the mental world of the psyche. There may even be a critical time for this, but, without the emotional bond that makes possible a personal empathic and essentially human relationship with another mind, intellectual growth and development can be fundamentally and seriously impaired.

Tustin's two themes—encapsulation and entanglement—describe, respectively, the states of autistic withdrawal and schizoid confusion. She saw autism as an extreme reaction to the "illusory trauma" of experiencing bodily separateness—the trauma that Mahler envisaged in the failure of symbiosis. As a reaction against what seemed to be felt as an "untimely" ejection from the psychological postnatal "womb", autistic withdrawal from human reality appears to be the final protective manoeuvre for survival: the child's human potential encased in the hard, uncaring crustacean exterior.

There is an intrinsic problem in trying to convey the quality of preverbal experience that prompts such drastic measures.

Fright comes close—a concept distinct from fear, which carries the notion of existence of an object to be feared. Fright, which includes shock and unexpectedness, is consistent with what is commonly understood by trauma. Primitive, preverbal experience, beyond the containment of words, has been described by Bion (1967, p. 116) as "nameless dread", which is probably the best description available for this primitive, atavistic fear. Bion's phrase conveys both the degree of terror and isolation involved and the total absence of any hope of salvation. Signally, Bion's description also contains the indication of the direction in which hope might lie—that is, in the civilizing potential of the name, were it to become available. Identification is the corollary of naming and is the prerequisite of differentiation and discrimination.

What is dreaded is the experience of uncontainment, of unboundedness in uncharted space. Winnicott has referred to a fear of "falling for ever" (1963a, p. 89; see also 1958, 1971) and links this to the primitive infantile fear of falling, which can at times be reactivated in falling asleep.

Autism is, for Tustin, a defence against the premature and unbearable awareness of the separateness and otherness of the object. She regards Kanner's syndrome (Kanner, 1943), Mahler's symbiotic psychosis, and what others have termed childhood schizophrenia as having in common one fundamentally autistic characteristic: their dislocation from reality, particularly the reality of other sentient beings.

It is important to appreciate the difference between loss of an object and loss of the possibility of contact with an object. The object has to have been found in order for its loss to be experienced—that is, the preconception of an object has to have found its realization (Bion, 1967; Green, 1983).

Tustin makes it clear, as does Mahler, that the void experienced by the children she describes is of a different order from loss of the object. A disruption that occurs between the pre-conception and its realization, between the innate expectation and the fulfilment, means that the loss is not something that is clear and meaningful but is the more deeply lost by being covered with confusion. Tustin finds in Winnicott's understanding of this catastrophic breakdown of contact something similar to her own clinical experience with autistic children.

Winnicott (1963b) says:

> For example, the loss might be that of certain aspects of the mouth which disappear from the infant's point of view along with the mother and the breast when there is separation at a date earlier than that at which the infant had reached a stage of emotional development which would provide the infant with the equipment for dealing with loss. The same loss of the mother a few months later would be a loss of object without this added element of a loss of part of the subject. [p. 222]

The term that Winnicott used for this *ultima Thule* of depressive experience is psychotic depression. It is the "black hole" or "pit" frequently referred to by depressed adult patients from which the possibility of a return feels to be in great peril.

In this world of blackness, hope has not been lost: it has been extinguished. The experience is often likened to falling into a bottomless pit—"I had to claw my way up again, inch by inch", said one patient.

# 4

## The child's relationship with the Other and with language: some concepts of Merleau-Ponty and Henri Wallon

In the language of Jean Piaget, it would be necessary for the child, at some point in his development, to learn to think in terms of reciprocity, to de-centre. I believe that for Piaget, to de-centre is to differentiate. Merleau-Ponty (1960) underlines that this process of de-centring is lived not only intellectually, but also emotionally. Perception of the outside world is profoundly modified by the child's personality and by his interpersonal relations. For the acquisition of language, there is also a close and profound connection between the development of language and interpersonal relations.

Language acquisition is a similar process to the child's relationship with his mother, a process of identification through which the subject projects onto the mother what he feels and incorporates his mother's attitudes. Learning to speak is learning to enact a series of roles, to assume a series of behaviours or linguistic gestures (Ciccone, 2011; Resnik 1973).

Merleau-Ponty underscores that the intellectual elaboration of our experience of the world is achieved through the elaboration of our human relations. The use of some linguistic instruments by the subject depends on the position the child adopts at each moment in the field of forces of the family and human environment that surrounds him. Hence, linguistic progress is explained by progress in the realm of affects.

I quote Merleau-Ponty (1960):

> The child's experience of his family constellation gives him more than a simple registry of certain relationships among human beings. The child learns a whole way of thinking, while he also assumes and informs his family relations. It is a complete use of language and at the same time, a way of perceiving the world. [p. 26]

Henri Wallon (1962), on the other hand, created the theory of the mirror—a concept original to this author. In it, he theorizes on the origin of identity and the creation of the body image. He underlines the importance of bodily interoception. These concepts are similar to those of Frances Tustin on the search for sensory stimulus. Moreover, these ideas on the concept of self, of "oneself" and identity, were later developed in detail by Winnicott (1971; see also De

Mijolla, 2001; Laplanche & Pontalis, 1973; Painceira Plot, 1997), in his theories of the true self and the false self.

The concept of identity is illustrated in the DVD when the boy not only says "I" but then adds, "I, Benjamin".

And I quote Shakespeare:

> If to do were as easy as to know what were good to do, chapels had been churches, and poor men's cottages princes' palaces. . . .
>
> *The Merchant of Venice*, Act I, Scene 2

# PART II

# BENJAMIN

# 5

# Testimonies

## The therapist

Benjamin, aged 3 years and 7 months, was brought to me by his mother for a consultation. She said he had been diagnosed at the Hospital Nacional Professor Alejandro Posadas, as well as at six other medical centres, as having a severe autism with no possibility of cure. "Absolutely no hope" was the conclusion from the previous seven medical consultations.

You will see his autistic behaviour in the first minutes of the film. He does not look at the eyes of the other people, he shouts and screams, he has tantrums, throws around all the toys off a small table, hits his head against the wall, and with no consciousness of danger climbs dangerously high places.

The mother told me that Benjamin had been well until he was about 2½ years old, when he developed severe autistic mechanisms following a traumatic event in the family: the sexual abuse of his sister, who was 6, by a teacher at her kindergarten.

From this time on, Benjamin started to isolate himself, to disconnect, to be aloof, to shout, to yell, to not sleep, and to bring any object to his mouth; he also didn't speak.

My initial thoughts were that the traumatic event—the sexual abuse of their daughter—had triggered the parents into being distraught with grief and anxiety. This had then provoked the boy to abruptly disconnect from his parents and his sister.

Up until this moment, he had had a very close and warm relationship with his sister, as you will see her say in the film.

I thought that Benjamin felt much the same way as did the poet Baudelaire, who had suffered a stroke and had lost the ability to speak. In one of his poems he wrote that he felt alone as if in the middle of the Sahara desert, unable to speak and with no one to listen to him.

During the eight years of Benjamin's treatment, which still continues today, both parents were always present. So I want to emphasize that the collaboration of the family with the psychoanalyst is of the utmost importance in the treatment of children with autistic mechanisms.

The family must work together with the psychoanalyst to take home with them what they learn

Hospital Nacional Prof. A. Posadas

Sección Neurología Infantil

Apellido y Nombre H.C.

Rp/ Benjamin , de 3 años 1 mes de edad padece de un trastorno generalizado del desarrollo de tipo autista con antecedentes de trastornos de alimentación y sueño en el primer año de vida, auto y heteroagresividad y ausencia de lenguaje con aislamiento a los dos años y medio, con EEG normal y RMI cerebral normal, aun no ha completado el plan de estudios. Se medicó con risperidona con mejoría de la atención y disminución de la agresión. Está en tratamiento psicoterapéutico.

1-7-03

Dra LIDIA PAULA CÁCERES
Neuróloga Infantil
MN 39804 MP 34878

Diagnostico Dra Caceres.
Hospital Posadas
1-7/2003.

Benjamin C. ______, 3 years 1 month old, suffers from a generalized developmental condition of an autistic nature, with a history of alimentary and sleep disorders during his first year of life. The patient exhibited self-harming behaviour and belligerence to others as well as absence of language and isolation at 2 years and 6 months of age. The EEG and the MRI brain-scan findings are normal. A study plan has not yet been completed. The patient was treated with Risperidone and has shown improved attention and decrease of aggressive behaviour. He is undergoing psychotherapeutic treatment.

1/07/03
Lidia Paula Cáceres, M.D., Paediatric Neurologist
MN 39804 – MP 34878

*Letter with diagnosis from the Department of Paediatric Neurology, Hospital Nacional Profesor Alejandro Posadas.*

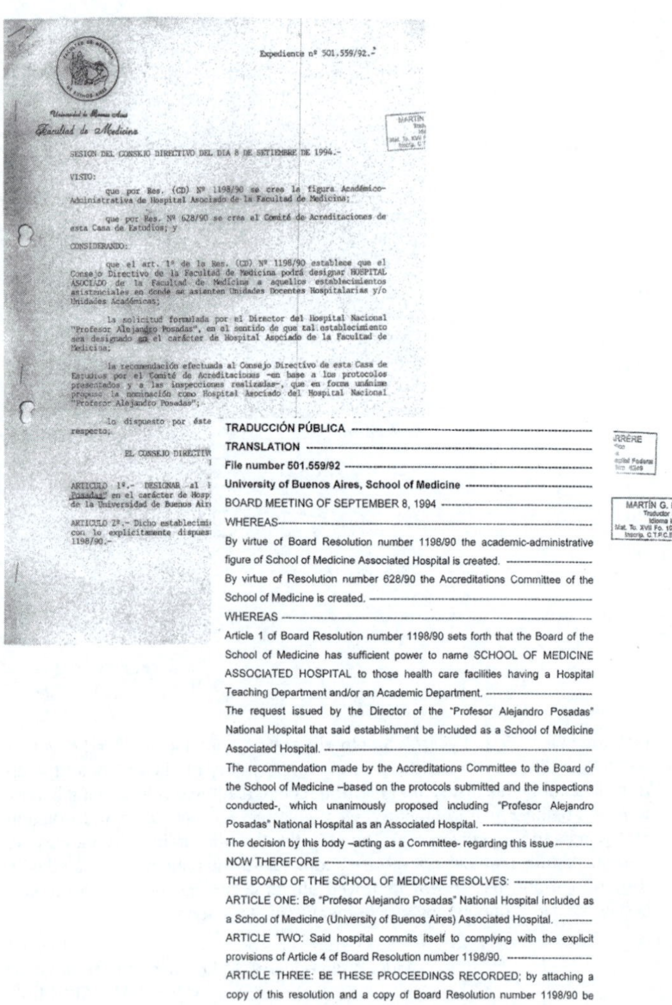

Universidad de Buenos Aires
Facultad de Medicina

Expediente nº 501.559/92.-

SESION DEL CONSEJO DIRECTIVO DEL DIA 8 DE SETIEMBRE DE 1994.-

VISTO:

que por Res. (CD) Nº 1198/90 se crea la figura Académico-Administrativa de Hospital Asociado de la Facultad de Medicina;

que por Res. Nº 628/90 se crea el Comité de Acreditaciones de esta Casa de Estudios; y

CONSIDERANDO:

que el art. 1º de la Res. (CD) Nº 1198/90 establece que el Consejo Directivo de la Facultad de Medicina podrá designar HOSPITAL ASOCIADO de la Facultad de Medicina a aquellos establecimientos asistenciales en donde se asienten Unidades Docentes Hospitalarias y/o Unidades Académicas;

la solicitud formulada por el Director del Hospital Nacional "Profesor Alejandro Posadas", en el sentido de que tal establecimiento sea designado en el carácter de Hospital Asociado de la Facultad de Medicina;

la recomendación efectuada al Consejo Directivo de esta Casa de Estudios por el Comité de Acreditaciones -en base a los protocolos presentados y a las inspecciones realizadas-, que en forma unánime propuso la nominación como Hospital Asociado del Hospital Nacional "Profesor Alejandro Posadas";-

lo dispuesto por éste
respecto;

EL CONSEJO DIRECTIV

ARTICULO 1º.- DESIGNAR al
Posadas" en el carácter de Hosp
de la Universidad de Buenos Air

ARTICULO 2º.- Dicho establecimi
con lo explícitamente dispues
1198/90.-

**TRADUCCIÓN PÚBLICA** ----------------------------------------

**TRANSLATION** ----------------------------------------

**File number 501.559/92** ----------------------------------------

**University of Buenos Aires, School of Medicine** ----------------------------------------

BOARD MEETING OF SEPTEMBER 8, 1994 ----------------------------------------

WHEREAS----------------------------------------

By virtue of Board Resolution number 1198/90 the academic-administrative figure of School of Medicine Associated Hospital is created. ----------------------

By virtue of Resolution number 628/90 the Accreditations Committee of the School of Medicine is created. ----------------------------------------

WHEREAS ----------------------------------------

Article 1 of Board Resolution number 1198/90 sets forth that the Board of the School of Medicine has sufficient power to name SCHOOL OF MEDICINE ASSOCIATED HOSPITAL to those health care facilities having a Hospital Teaching Department and/or an Academic Department. ----------------------------

The request issued by the Director of the "Profesor Alejandro Posadas" National Hospital that said establishment be included as a School of Medicine Associated Hospital. ----------------------------------------

The recommendation made by the Accreditations Committee to the Board of the School of Medicine –based on the protocols submitted and the inspections conducted-, which unanimously proposed including "Profesor Alejandro Posadas" National Hospital as an Associated Hospital. ----------------------------

The decision by this body –acting as a Committee- regarding this issue----------

NOW THEREFORE ----------------------------------------

THE BOARD OF THE SCHOOL OF MEDICINE RESOLVES: --------------------

ARTICLE ONE: Be "Profesor Alejandro Posadas" National Hospital included as a School of Medicine (University of Buenos Aires) Associated Hospital. ---------

ARTICLE TWO: Said hospital commits itself to complying with the explicit provisions of Article 4 of Board Resolution number 1198/90. ----------------------

ARTICLE THREE: BE THESE PROCEEDINGS RECORDED; by attaching a copy of this resolution and a copy of Board Resolution number 1198/90 be

*Official accreditation document of the Hospital Nacional Profesor Alejandro Posadas as a School of Medicine of the University of Buenos Aires, with certified translation.*

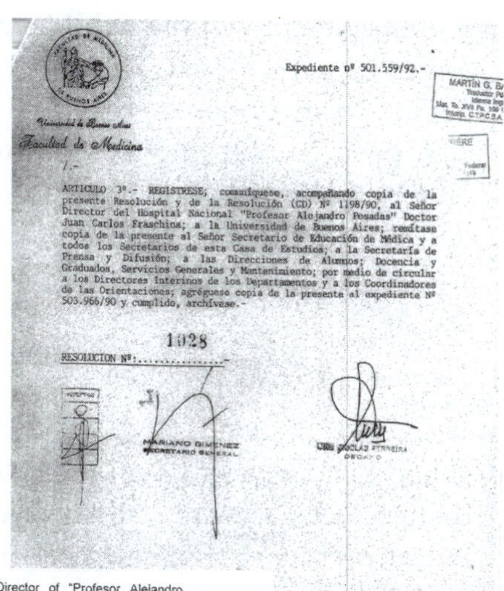

Universidad de Buenos Aires

Facultad de Medicina

Expediente nº 501.559/92.-

/.-

ARTICULO 3º.- REGISTRESE; comuníquese, acompañando copia de la presente Resolución y de la Resolución (CD) Nº 1198/90, al Señor Director del Hospital Nacional "Profesor Alejandro Posadas" Doctor Juan Carlos Fraschina; a la Universidad de Buenos Aires; remítase copia de la presente al Señor Secretario de Educación de Médica y a todos los Secretarios de esta Casa de Estudios; a la Secretaría de Prensa y Difusión; a las Direcciones de Alumnos; Docencia y Graduados, Servicios Generales y Mantenimiento; por medio de circular a los Directores Interinos de los Departamentos y a los Coordinadores de las Orientaciones; agréguese copia de la presente al expediente Nº 503.966/90 y cumplido, archívese.-

RESOLUCION Nº: 1028.-

MARIANO GIMENEZ
SECRETARIO GENERAL

DECANO

these proceedings communicated to the Director of "Profesor Alejandro Posadas" National Hospital, Doctor Juan Carlos Fraschina; to the University of Buenos Aires. Be a copy of these proceedings delivered to the Secretary of Medical Education of the School of Medicine and to all other Secretaries of this University, to the Department of Press and Outreach, to the Department of Students; to the Faculty and Graduates Departments, to General Services and Maintenance Departments; and by virtue of a circular letter be these proceedings delivered to Acting Directors of the Departments and to Coordinators of Orientation Units; be a copy of these proceedings attached to file number 503.966/90. Once completed, be these proceedings filed. ----------

RESOLUTION NUMBER 1028 ----------

[There appears a signature] MARIANO GIMENEZ, SECRETARY GENERAL ---

[There appears a signature] LUIS NICOLÁS FERREIRA, DEAN ----------

**THIS IS A TRUE AND ACCURATE TRANSLATION INTO THE ENGLISH LANGUAGE OF THE DOCUMENT (PHOTOCOPY) WRITTEN IN THE SPANISH LANGUAGE, ATTACHED HERETO, BUENOS AIRES OCTOBER 7, 2011** ----------

***For legalization purposes by the Colegio de Traductores Públicos de la Ciudad de Buenos Aires [Association of Sworn Translators of the City of Buenos Aires]*** ----------

**ES TRADUCCIÓN FIEL Y COMPLETA AL IDIOMA INGLÉS DEL DOCUMENTO (FOTOCOPIA) REDACTADO EN IDIOMA ESPAÑOL, QUE SE ADJUNTA, BUENOS AIRES 7 DE OCTUBRE DE 2011** ----------

**SE EXTIENDE EN DOS FOJAS NUMERADAS** ----------

MARTÍN G. BARRÈRE
Traductor Público
Idioma Inglés
Mat. To. XVII Fo. 100 Capital Federal
Inscrip. C.T.P.C.B.A. Nro. 6249

and discover about their child's mental mechanisms, which is very clearly shown in my interpretations during the treatment.

A positive outcome to such treatment is possible only in the presence of—and only if there is—a close-knit family who help the therapist and are able to contain and understand the mental mechanisms of the child.

## The mother

When Benjamin was about 2 years old, he had sleep disturbances, severe eating disorders, and behavioural problems. The diagnosis of autism was later given to us after he had been to several health centres and to Posadas Hospital.

All the doctors diagnosed him as having severe autism and severe emotional disturbances. He was sent to an educational centre where we were told he would never be able to speak. He would never play. This diagnosis indicated a situation that was impossible to reverse.

He was over-medicated; at the age of 3 years, he suffered a panic crisis. He was over-medicated again with three other new drugs. This was counterproductive, and he became worse. He had a more acute crisis.

Before he was 4 years old, we were still searching for other alternatives and further consultations, but each time we received the same diagnosis. They all said this was irreversible, and we were given the same bad prognosis. They told us that the only thing that differentiated him from an animal was that he could say a couple of words.

But then we went to Dr David, whose name I had heard at a conference. David told us that Benjamin was not as ill as all the doctors had said. Imagine—those doctors had said there was no hope of him recovering!

Today, Benjamin is at a normal, standard school, in first grade. He is going almost all the hours a normal kid is supposed to go. And he is doing almost the same subjects, the same content, and the same activities as the other students.

Benjamin is on the road to being like the other kids. Today his relationship with the other children is good; he is not aggressive, he speaks using many words, and he is understood more easily.

## The father

It all started just before Benjamin was 3, after his little sister had been sexually abused at the kindergarten. He was blocked, a total block of language and behaviour. I had not understood this until we spoke to Dr David. Benjamin didn't sleep, couldn't talk or play. It was all getting worse.

He hit his head against the wall, he was fearless, he climbed on anything, he didn't restrain himself, and he couldn't control himself. He didn't eat well. He didn't smile. He didn't speak at all.

Then later, when we started with Dr David, there

was a change. A great change. And together with Dr David we also learnt how to deal with him. Thank God, Benjamin today acts as you will see in the video. He is now in the first year of primary school, and he performs the same activities as any other child in primary school.

# 6

## Transformation

This chapter contains selected scenes from the DVD, *"Now I Am a Real Kid": Treatment of Autism,* attached to this book, showing Benjamin's transformation over years of treatment from a severely disturbed child with autism into "a real kid".

**1**

Benjamin at the age of 3 years, knocking his head against the wall. At this time, he doesn't sleep, doesn't smile, doesn't talk, doesn't make eye contact, and has no notion of danger.

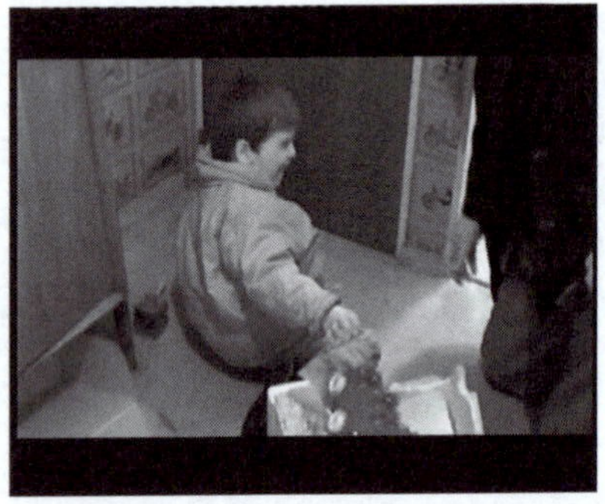

**2**

He throws toys onto the floor, then throws himself down, shouts at the therapist, and hits out.

3

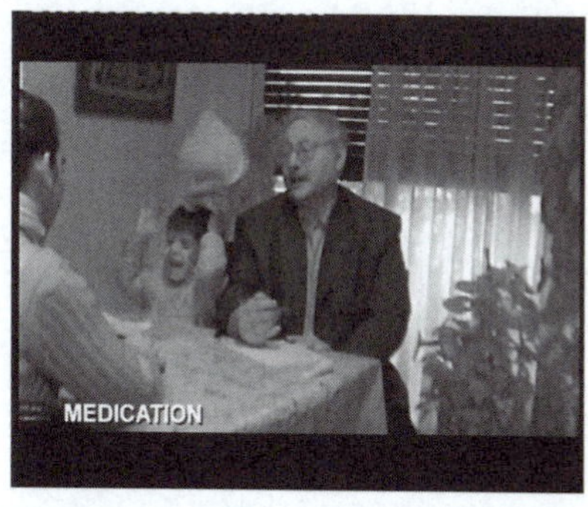


An expression of terror comes over his face. He throws a piece of paper and then tears it into pieces.

4

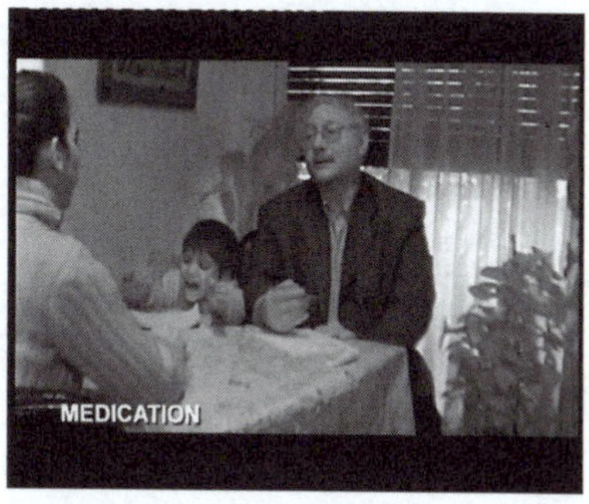


His face as he is screaming; he is suffering. *He needs medication.*

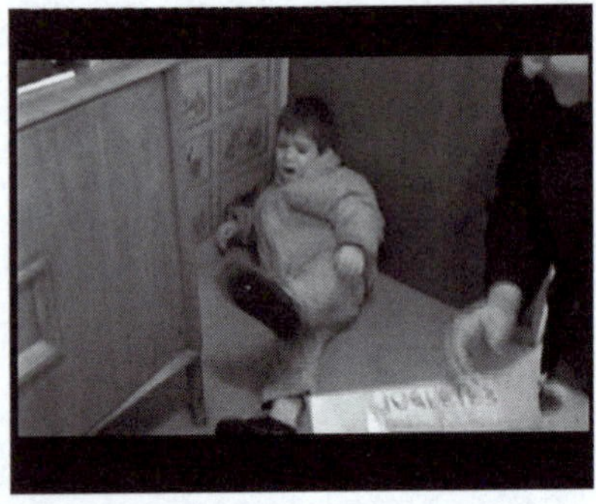

5

The child went on like this for months, shouting, sobbing, unable to sleep, kicking, punching, and knocking his head against the walls and doors of the therapist's office.

6

After seven months of treatment, improvements begin to appear. He puts the chess pieces into the box. For the first time he puts toys into a box—the inauguration of the creation of a mental space for containment. He still does not make eye contact.

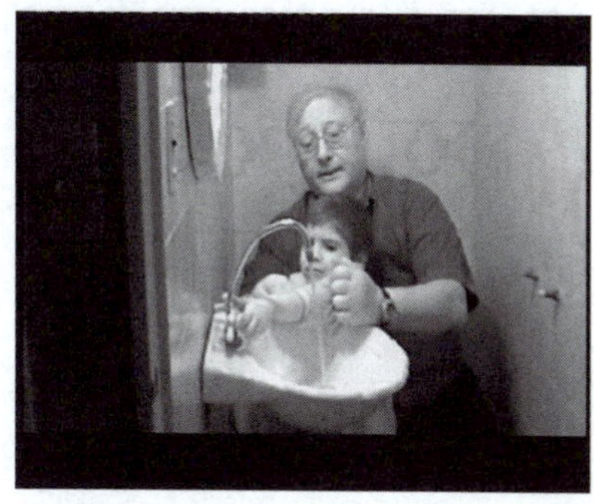

7

He accepts being held in my arms for the first time, in the bathroom, playing with water.

8

After the child touches sensorily, the therapist adds the verbal symbol, "water". Some time later, this is the first word he says, but only after making sensory contact. *This is more than a year into treatment.*

9

He plays with the xylophone and doesn't throw toys on the floor.

10

He learns to fit pieces together, to fill in the empty spaces with the animal that belongs in each space.

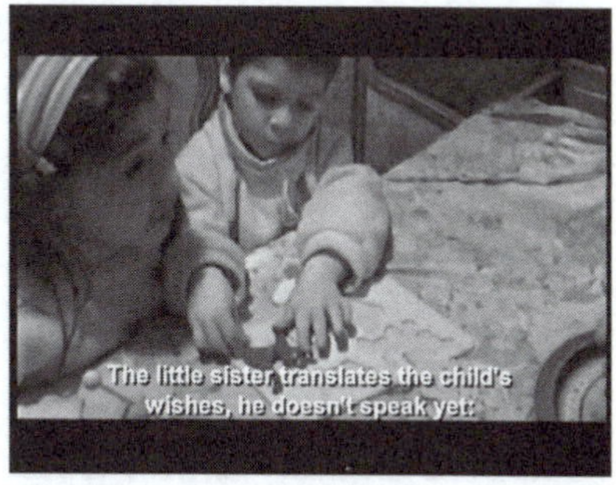


**11**

His sister translates his wishes—he doesn't speak yet.

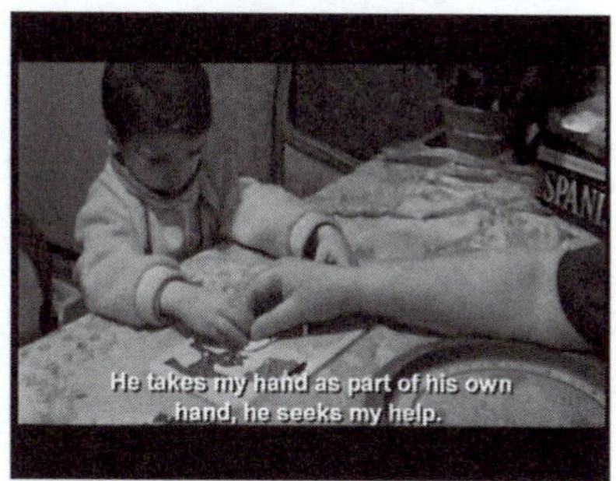


**12**

He takes my hand as part of his own hand, seeking my help.

**13**

He makes contact with a cassette using his tongue and the mucous membrane of his lips. When he makes sensory contact with the object, the therapist adds the verbal symbol: "cassette". The child doesn't use distal eye and ear perception.

**14**

He touches a book with his hands and mouth: sensory contact. The therapist gives it a name, or symbol, by saying the word "book" and gives a name to each object the child touches. The child's mental apparatus has to be recreated.

From sensory contact to word-representation and verbal symbols—the language used is the symbol for each object he touches, to which the therapist gives words. Only in these conditions can a child recover what was locked inside autistic encapsulation.

**15**

He still cries and hits.

**16**

He doesn't mix the white chess pieces with the black ones. The creation of mental spaces is improving—there is differentiation and individuation.

**17**

He recreates his own body image, which he imagines as torn apart.

**18**

He takes his sister's hand and uses it to point at a drawing. Then, his sister says: "camel". Symbiosis can be seen here. A verbal symbol is created: the word "camel".

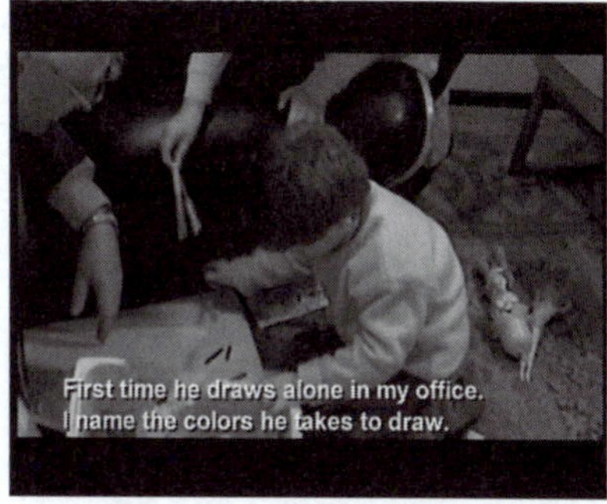


**19**

The first time he draws by himself in my office. I give names to the colours he uses. His sister translates: she gives the name. She says, "He's drawing an animal."

**20**

He starts to smile. A mental space between mother and child is created: the space of illusion (Winnicott). What was hidden and well preserved in autistic encapsulation inside his mind reappears. There is a musical dialogue between mother and child through babble: useful and healthy symbiosis (Mahler), the introjection and projection of one inside the other (Klein). The sound of the mother's voice envelops the child (Anzieu). Mother's eyes are like a mirror answering the child (Winnicott).

**21**

His mother reads a biography of Baudelaire. It tells how Baudelaire's mother had taught him to speak and to recover words after the poet had had a cerebrovascular accident during a trip from Brussels to Paris.

**22**

The therapist reads the story of Pinocchio while Benjamin listens attentively.

23

For the first time there is the symbolic creation of a game and a mental space that can be introjected. He invents a game with objects on the therapist's desk: *he creates an imaginary car, with pencils and marker pens as passengers.*

24

He feeds the cow chocolate while playing with the farm animals—a nutritive oral relation. He no longer makes the animals fight each other; now he feeds them.

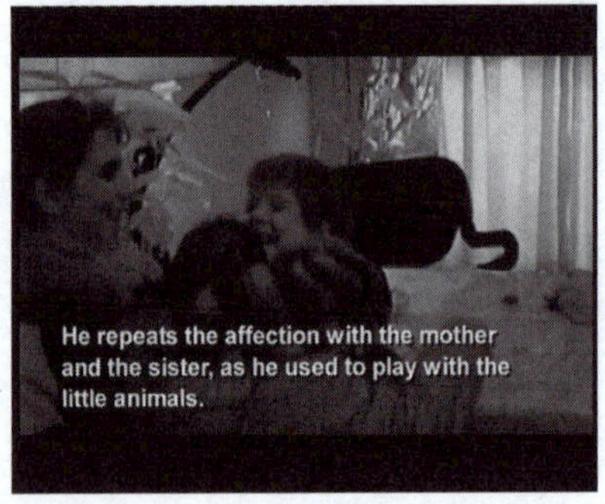


**25**

A hug with his sister and his mother. He repeats the affection with his mother and sister that he used previously when playing with the toy animals.

**26**

The most important game—hide and seek, appearing and disappearing (peek-a-boo). Three years ago he would have screamed, believing that people had disappeared and died. He can now play at something that used to terrify him.

27

Music therapy. Learning a melody is equivalent to learning a complete and linguistically well-structured phrase. Rhythm and body movement are also mental growth.

28

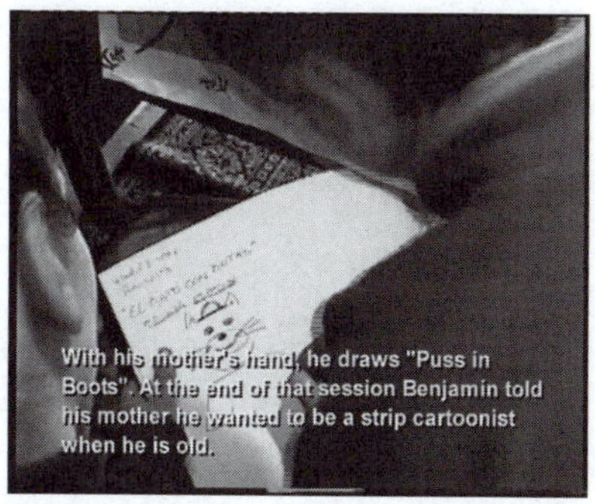


He draws "Puss in Boots". In this session Benjamin says that when he is bigger he wants to draw comic strips. Today, several years later, this boy invents and draws his own characters that he uses to tell stories.

**29**

Benjamin talks about Pinocchio and about Gepetto, who takes care of Pinocchio. Benjamin leans back on the therapist.

**30**

Three and a half years into treatment: the boy speaks to his father.

**31**

Benjamin reads. The autistic encapsulation is open: suddenly all his mental capacities emerge, among them the ability to read. He reads the titles of children's stories and fairy tales. He has a global perception of words.

**32**

He reads "Puss in Boots", "Sleeping Beauty", "Little Red Riding Hood", "Three Little Pigs", "Cinderella", . . .

**33**

Benjamin says that Benjamin-Pinocchio is dead. "I'm not Pinocchio any more—I'm Benjamin", because he now goes to kindergarten and can play and has friends. He says that he goes to a kindergarten for real children.

**34**

His parents tell me that Benjamin has graduated to first grade. Benjamin says that he is like the story of "The Turtle [Tortoise] and the Hare", but that he is the Turtle: he is coming to the end of the race.

**35**

Benjamin's graduate T-shirt after graduating from kindergarten. He also received an award for *imagination* given by all the teachers at school for creating the best stories—an award and a graduation diploma!

**36**

In the school grounds with the flag. A very *humble* [i.e., modest] school.

37

Benjamin's first copy book at primary school: the work is done well.

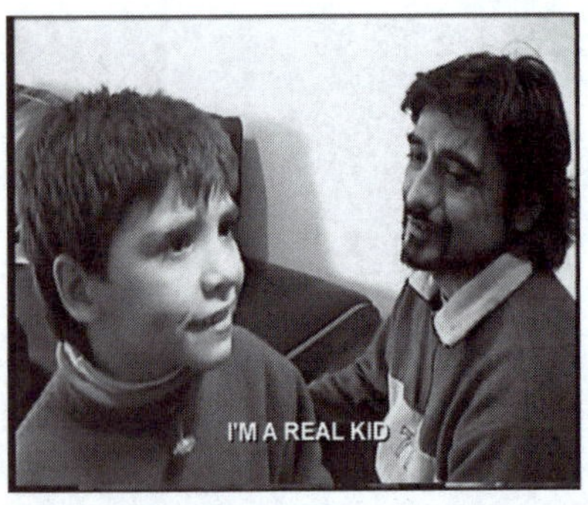


38

Benjamin says: "I'm a real kid."

# References


Avenburg, R. (1995). *Breve historia del pensamiento de Freud*. Buenos Aires: Editorial Claridad.

Bion, W. R. (1967). *Second Thoughts*. London: Karnac, 1984.

Ciccone, A. (2011). *La psychanalyse à l'épreuve du bébé*. Paris: Dunod.

De Mijolla, A. (2001). *Dictionnaire de la psychanalyse*. Paris: Calmann-Levy.

Ferrari, P. (1987). Enfants présentant une problématique abandonnique. *Journal de la Psychanalyse de l'Enfant: Le Transfert, 4*.

Freud, S. (1891). *On Aphasia*. New York: International Universities Press, 1953.

Freud, S. (1900). *The Interpretation of Dreams. Standard Edition, 5*.

Freud, S. (1911). Formulations on the two principles of mental functioning. *Standard Edition, 12*.

Freud, S. (1926 [1925]). *Inhibitions, Symptoms and Anxiety. Standard Edition, 20.*

Freud, S. (1950 [1895]). Project for a scientific psychology. *Standard Edition, 1.*

Green, A. (1983). *Narcissisme de vie, narcissisme de mort.* Paris: Editions de Minuit.

Grotstein, J. (1978). Inner space: Its dimensions and its coordinates. *International Journal of Psychoanalysis, 59*: 55–61.

Grubrich-Simitis, I. (2003). *Zurück zu Freuds Texten. Stumme Dokumente sprechen machen.* Frankfurt am Main: Fischer Verlag.

Haesler, L. (1992). Modes of transgenerational transmission of the trauma of Nazi persecution and their appearance in treatment. *Journal of Social Work and Policy in Israel, 5/6.*

Haesler, L. (2010). *"Shall Hate Be Fairer Lodg'd Gentle Love?" Struggling for Survival and Autonomy.* Paper presented at the 5th Frances Tustin Memorial Conference, Berlin.

Houzel, D. (2000). Le traumatisme de la naissance. In: C. Geissmann & D. Houzel (Eds.), *L'enfant, ses parents et le psychanalyste.* Paris: Bayard.

Houzel, D., & Bursztejn, C. (2000). Autisme infantile. In: D. Houzel, M. Emmanuelli, & F. Moggio (Eds.), *Dictionnaire de psychopathologie de l'enfant et de l'adolescent.* Paris: Presses Universitaires de France.

Kanner, L. (1943). Autistic disturbance of affective contact. *The Nervous Child,* 2: 217–50. Reprinted in: *Childhood Psychosis: Initial Studies and New Insights*. New York: Wiley, 1973.

Laplanche, J., & Pontalis, J.-B. (1973). *The Language of Psychoanalysis.* London: Karnac, 1998.

Levi Montalcini, R. (2009). Rita Levy Montalcini, Nobel-Prize winning Scientist turns 100, still working. *The Huffington Post*, 18 April.

Mahler, M., Pine, F., & Bergman, A. (1975). *The Psychological Birth of the Human Infant: Symbiosis and Individuation*. New York: Basic Books, 2000.

Merleau-Ponty, M. (1960). *Les relations avec autrui chez l'enfant*. Paris: Centre de Documentation Universitaire, Sorbonne.

Nissen, B. (Ed.) (2006). *Autistische Phänomene in psychoanalytischen Behandlungen*. Giessen: Psychosozial-Verlag.

Painceira Plot, A. (1997). *Clínica psicoanalítica a partir de la obra de Winnicott*. Buenos Aires: Editorial Lumen.

Resnik, S. (1973). *Personne et psychose*. Paris: Payot.

Rosenfeld, D. (1986). Identification and its vicissitudes in relation to the Nazi phenomenon. In: *The Psychotic: Aspects of the Personality*. London: Karnac, 1992.

Rosenfeld, D. (1992). *The Psychotic: Aspects of the Personality*. London: Karnac.

Rosenfeld, D. (2006). *The Soul, the Mind, and the Psychoanalyst*. London: Karnac. [German edition, *Die Seele, die Psyche und der Analytiker*. Giessen: Psychosozial-Verlag, 2008. French edition, *L'âme, le psychisme et le psychanalyste*. Larmor-Plage: Editions du Hublot, 2010.]

Spensley, S. (1995). Encapsulation and entanglement (2nd revised edition). In: *Frances Tustin: Makers of Modern Psychotherapy*. London: Routledge, 1994.

Tustin, F. (1986). *Autistic Barriers in Neurotic Patients* (2nd revised edition). London: Karnac, 1994.

Tustin, F. (1990). *The Protective Shell in Children and Adults*. London: Karnac.

Wallon, H. (1962). Espace postural et espace environnant (le schéma corporel). *Enfance, 15* (1): 1–33.

Winnicott, D. W. (1958). *Collected Papers: Through Paediatrics to Psychoanalysis*. [Revised edition: *Through Paediatrics to Psychoanalysis: Collected Papers*. London: Hogarth Press, 1975; reprinted London: Karnac, 1984.]

Winnicott, D. W. (1963a). Fear of breakdown. In: *Psychoanalytic Explorations* (pp. 87–95). London: Karnac, 1989.

Winnicott, D. W. (1963b). The mentally ill in your caseload. In: *The Maturational Processes and the Facilitating Environment*. London: Hogarth Press, 1965; reprinted London: Karnac, 1990.

Winnicott, D. W. (1970). I. Basis for self in body. *International Journal of Child Psychotherapy, 1* (No. 1, 1972). Reprinted in: *Psychoanalytic Explorations* (pp. 261–271). London: Karnac, 1989.

# Index